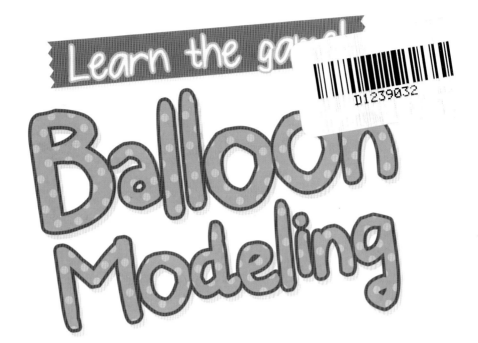

Learn the game!

Balloon Modeling

TOP THAT

Licensed exclusively to Top That Publishing Ltd
Tide Mill Way, Woodbridge, Suffolk, IP12 1AP, UK
www.topthatpublishing.com
Copyright © 2014 Tide Mill Media
All rights reserved
0 2 4 6 8 9 7 5 3 1
Printed and bound in China

Practical Tips

Totally amazing balloon animals are easy and great fun to make. Here are some basic tips to get you started.

What kind of balloons?

You can buy modeling balloons from most toy or hobby stores. The models in this book use balloons 11 3/4 in. long. Fully inflated, they could become five times their size.

How much air?

Balloons are easiest to work if they are only half-full of air. If you fill them with too much air, they might burst. Follow the instructions for each model carefully.

How should I inflate the balloon?

Use a balloon pump. You can buy one from a toy store or online. Pump the air in until your balloon reaches the length you need. Remove the pump, then tie the balloon off with an overhand knot.

How important are measurements?

Measurements given for bubble lengths are just a guide to help you start. Once you get the hang of them, you can develop the models in any way you want!

Do the twist!

All balloon animals are made from sausage-shaped bubbles: pinched, twisted and held together by the stretch of the balloon and the tension between the bubbles—magic! Learn these basic twists and you'll soon be making models of every shape and size.

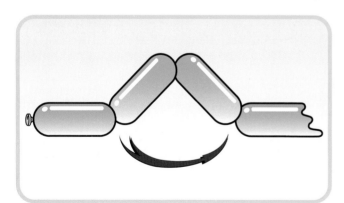

Lock Twist

A twist is two full turns of the balloon. Once you have made one bubble, you must not let go until you have made two more to twist together and "lock" in place.

Ear Twist

The second bubble is bent right over and double-twisted at the point where it joins the first.

Practice Makes Pefect

Take time to practice these basic steps before
you start on a model. Use a balloon blown up to 17 ³/₄ in.
The colors suggested are just a guide—choose your
favorite colors for each model.

1. Hold the balloon with your left hand at the
knotted end. Pinch the balloon about 4 in. from the
knot with your first finger and thumb.

2. Twist the rest of the balloon twice with your
right hand. Hold the twist tightly.

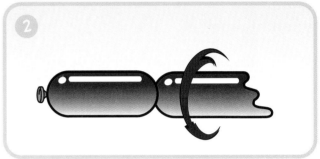

3. Slide your right hand along the balloon a further
4 in. Make another pinch and double twist.

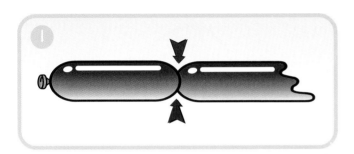

4. Fold the balloon over at this second twist.
Hold it in place with your left thumb and finger.

5. Slide your right hand along the balloon
again and pinch another 4 in. bubble. Make
another double twist.

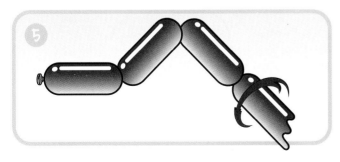

6. Hold the first twist and the last twist together
firmly with your left hand. Twist the two middle
bubbles twice to lock them together.

Practise drawing features onto your animals—use permanent felt-tip pens if you
have them. Be careful not to get any on your clothes or your surroundings!

Squeaky Mouse

Some very small bubbles make up this little character.
You will need to squeeze the air out of some of them before you
twist, so that they are only half as fat as the main balloon.

1. Begin with a balloon inflated to just 7 3/4 in. Squeeze and twist a 2 in. bubble for the head.

2. Squeeze and twist a 1 1/4 in. bubble and ear twist it to the head.

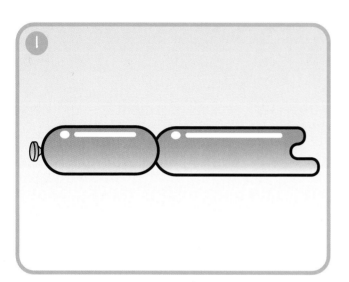

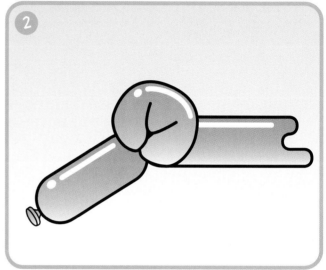

3. Squeeze and twist another 1 1/4 in. bubble. Ear twist it next to the first. Hold the balloon knot and tug it down and around to make the head bubble curve and look more mouse-like.

4. Squeeze and twist a 3/4 in. bubble to make the neck and two more 3/4 in. bubbles for the front legs. Lock twist the legs together next to the neck.

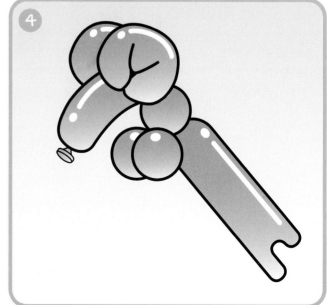

5. Squeeze and twist a 1 ¼ in. bubble for the body and two ¾ in. bubbles for the back legs.

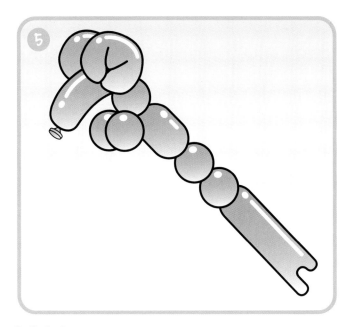

6. Lock twist the legs together behind the body. You should have a small bubble about ¾ in. and a long piece of balloon left over to be the mouse's tail. Add facial features with a felt-tip pen.

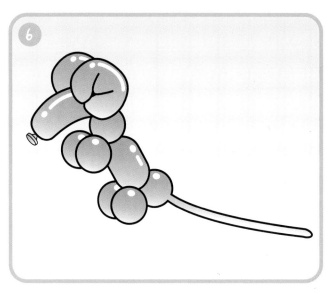

Squeak! Squeak!

To make your mouse come alive, use a black felt-tip pen to add a nose, mouth and whiskers.

Cool Dog

Fido here takes just one
balloon inflated to 23 ½ in.

1. Make two 3 ¾ in. bubbles at the knotted end of the balloon. Fold the second bubble over and ear twist it to make a nose and ears.

2. Make three 3 ¼ in. bubbles along the balloon. Lock the first and third twists together to make a neck and two front legs.

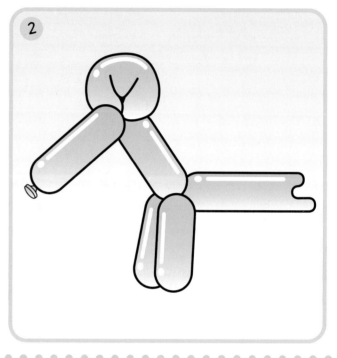

3. Make three more bubbles: 4 in. and two 3 ¼ in. Lock the first and third twists together for a body and back legs. Turn the back legs so that they line up with the front ones.

The remaining part of the balloon will form Fido's tail. Draw details with a black felt-tip pen to complete your cool dog.

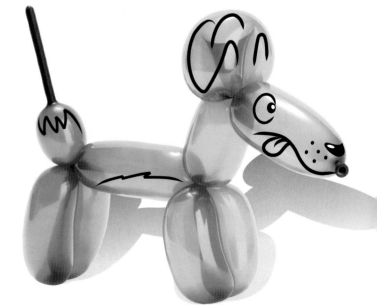

Beautiful Hummingbird

This neat little hummingbird is really easy,
use a balloon inflated to 31 ½ in.

1. Twist one 2 in. bubble at the knotted end for the body, then one 2 ¼ in. bubble at the other end for the head. The long piece of uninflated balloon will form the bird's beak.

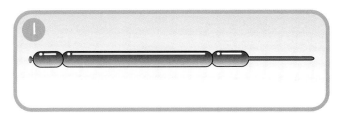

2. Bend the middle bubble over and lock twist the head and tail together. This should give you a large loop.

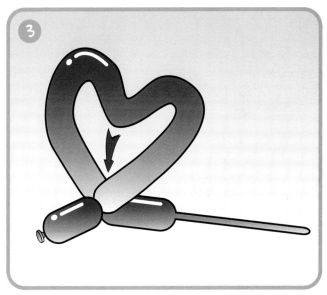

3. Pinch the center of the loop, press down and lock twist it to the neck to form the wings.

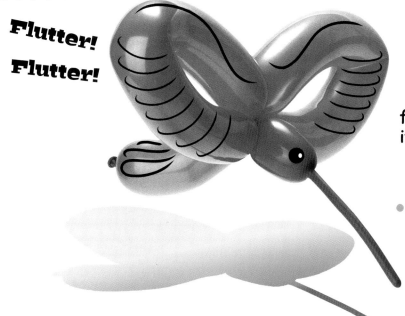

Flutter!
Flutter!

Finish your model with a face, and some feathers on its back. For a more exotic look, use glitter pens to decorate the wings.

Pony

You'll need two balloons to complete this model.
It looks great with a contrasting body and mane!

1. Inflate a balloon, leaving a 6 in. tip. Tie a knot in the end. Starting from the knotted end, make the head with a 2 ¼ in. bubble. Ear twist a 1 in. bubble, and then repeat with another to make the ears.

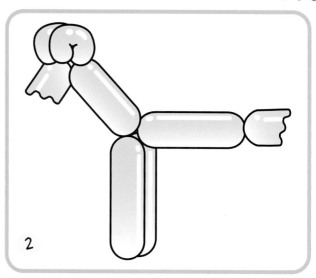

2. Twist a 2 ¼ in. bubble to make the neck. Now twist two 4 in. bubbles and lock twist them to make the front legs. Twist a 4 in. bubble to make the body.

3. To form the back legs, twist two more 4 in. bubbles and lock twist them together.

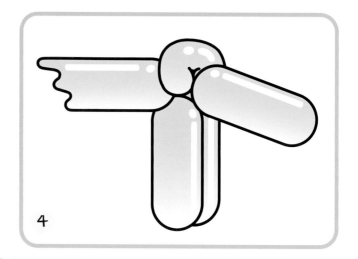

4. Push the rest of the balloon down between the back legs. Ear twist a ¾ in. bubble to hold the tail in position.

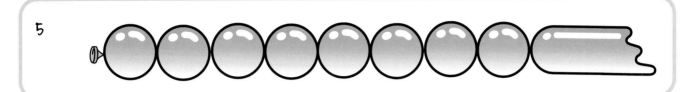

5

5. To make the pony's mane, inflate the second balloon to 7 ¾ in. in length. Tie a knot in the end. Starting from the knotted end, twist a chain of eight ¾ in. bubbles. Hold the chain firmly!

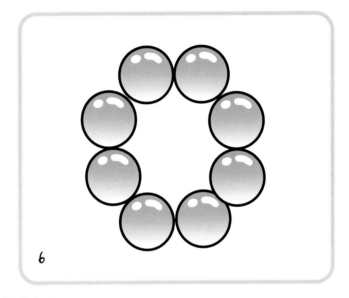

6

6. Tie a knot after the last bubble, and then tie the two knots of the bubble chain to make a ring. Deflate the rest of the balloon and save the scrap piece for the next step.

Add detail with a black felt-tip pen to give your pony real character!

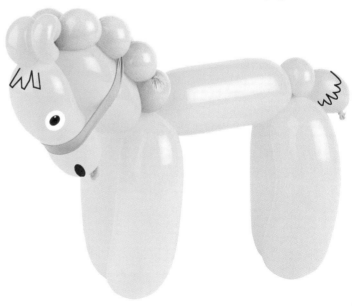

7

7. Put the ring on the pony's forehead so it hangs in front of its chest. Push back the bubbles at the top of the head and at the base of the neck to form a double row of bubbles along the back of the neck. Take the balloon scrap and tie it around the pony's nose and neck to keep the mane in position.

Playful, Purring Cat

This model is tricky, so you might need some help!
Squeeze the bubbles as you twist to make them easier to work.

1. Begin with a balloon inflated to 27 1/2 in. Twist a 4 in. bubble for the nose and a 2 1/4 in. bubble for the cat's cheek.

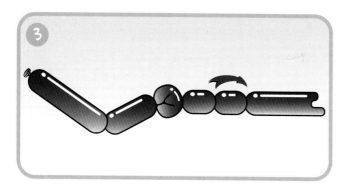

2. Hold on to the first bubble while you squeeze and twist a 1 1/4 in. bubble for an ear. Bend the ear bubble over and ear twist it to the cheek.

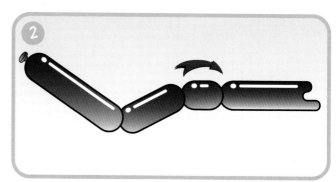

3. Twist a 1 1/4 in. bubble for the top of the cat's head. Squeeze and twist another 1 1/4 in. ear bubble. Bend it over and ear twist it to the head.

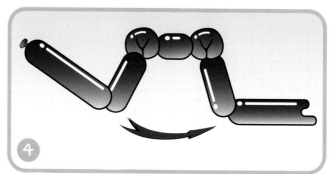

4. Twist another 2 1/4 in. cheek bubble. Lock twist it to the nose.

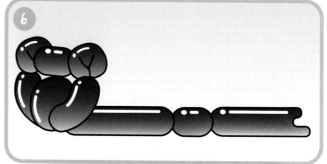

5. Bend the nose bubble over and push it between the cat's cheeks. Pull down the knot and tie it to the neck.

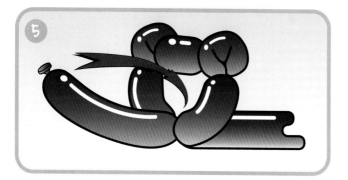

6. Now twist a 4 in. bubble to make a front leg. Then squeeze and twist a 1 1/4 in. bubble to make a paw.

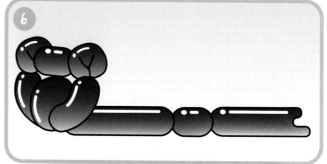

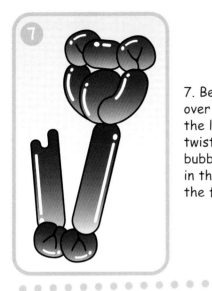

7. Bend the paw bubble over and ear twist to the leg. Squeeze and twist another 1 1/4 in. bubble and ear twist it in the same place as the first.

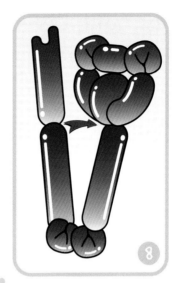

8. Twist another 4 in. front leg. Lock twist it to the back of the head.

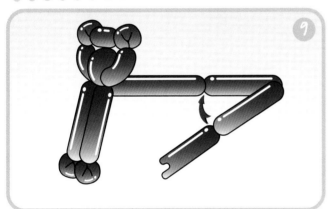

9. Next, twist a 6 in. bubble to make the cat's body. Twist two 4 in. back legs. Fold them over and lock twist to the body.

10. Bring the back legs forward and join them to the paws with a tiny piece of tape.

Purr!

Purr!

Squeeze the air down the remaining length of balloon to make the tail. Finish your cat with nose, eyes and whiskers drawn in felt-tip pen.

Graceful Swan

This model takes two balloons. Use white for a classic swan, or black for a more exotic variety.

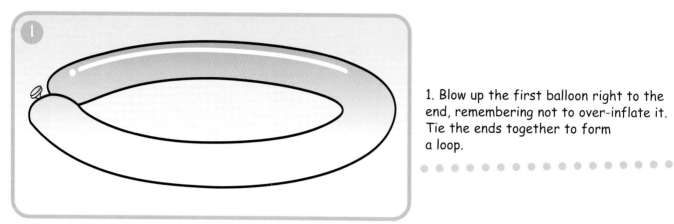

1. Blow up the first balloon right to the end, remembering not to over-inflate it. Tie the ends together to form a loop.

2. Twist the loop into a figure eight, keeping the knot at one end. You should now have two rings: one plain and one with a knot.

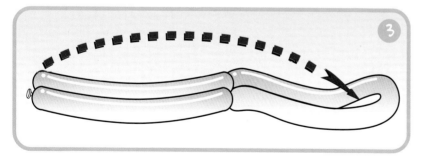

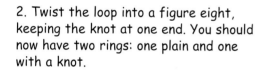

3. Bend the rings to make them curve. Bring the knotted ring over to tuck underneath the second ring.

4. Blow up a second balloon to 35 1/2 in. Make a 6 in. bubble at the knotted end to form a tail.

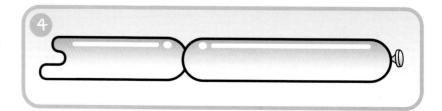

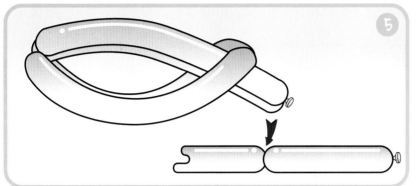

5. Lock twist the tail bubble at the knot in the first balloon.

6. Twist a 7 $\frac{3}{4}$ in. bubble in the second balloon to make the body. Lock twist it to the join of the two rings in the first balloon. The remaining bubble will form the swan's neck and head.

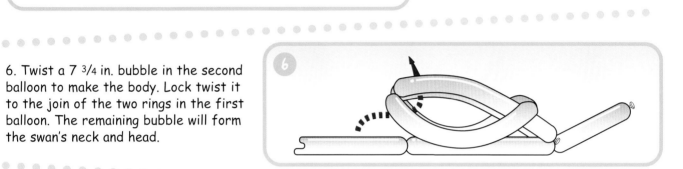

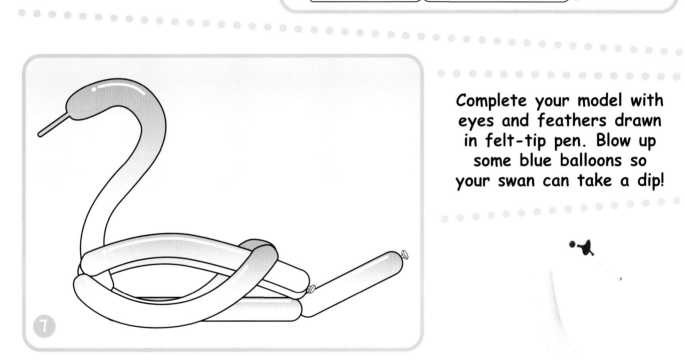

7. Pinch the top and base of the neck tightly with two hands. Roll and bend the neck until it is a nice "S" shape.

Complete your model with eyes and feathers drawn in felt-tip pen. Blow up some blue balloons so your swan can take a dip!

Leaf-lovin' Giraffe

This gentle giant uses a balloon inflated to 29 ½ in. Take special care when working the small bubbles for its ears— squeeze out some air if necessary.

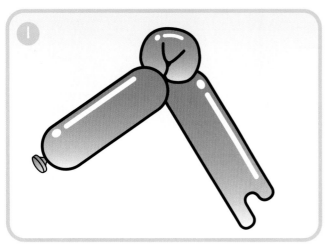

1. Twist a 3 ¾ in. bubble at the knotted end for the head. Now twist a 1 ½ in. bubble. Fold it back to the head and ear twist the two together.

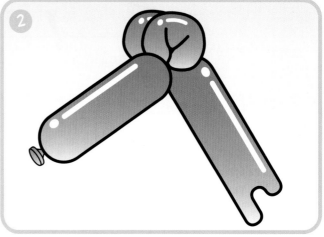

2. Twist another 1 ½ in. bubble for the second ear. Bend this back in the same way as for the first and ear twist it in place behind the head.

3. Now twist one 6 ¾ in. bubble for the neck and two 4 in. bubbles for the front legs. Lock twist the front legs together.

4. Twist a 2 ¼ in. bubble for the body and two 3 ¼ in. bubbles for the back legs. Lock twist the back legs together.

5. You should have a small bubble left in the balloon to be the tail. Tidy the shape of your giraffe to make it stand straight and pull the tail downward.

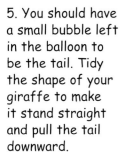

Munch! Munch!

Complete your model by drawing a face and patches down the neck and along the back.

Very Hungry Crocodile

To make this snappy chap, squeeze some air out of the smaller bubbles before you twist (this makes them easier to work). They need half the amount of air of the larger bubbles.

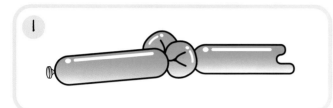

1. Blow up a balloon to 13 ¾ in. Twist a 4 in. bubble from the knotted end for the face. Squeeze and twist a 2 in. bubble for one eye. Bend the eye bubble back and ear twist it to the head. Ear twist another 2 in. bubble for the second eye.

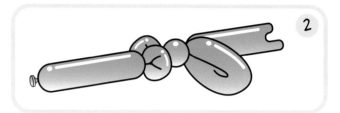

2. Squeeze and twist a 1 ¼ in. bubble for the neck. Twist a 6 in. bubble for the first leg. Bend this bubble over and ear twist it behind the neck.

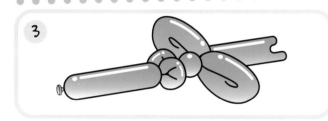

3. Now twist a second 6 in. leg bubble. Bend it over and ear twist it in the same place as the first so they sit side by side.

This is how your crocodile should look at this stage. Straighten the legs to sit flat behind the head.

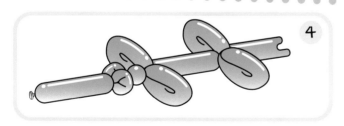

4. Twist a 4 in. bubble for the body and a 6 in. bubble for one back leg. Bend this over and ear twist it behind the body. Make another 6 in. bubble and ear twist it in the same way, to make the second leg. Straighten the legs to lie flat.

5. You'll have a small bubble left over. Squeeze the air along the remaining piece of balloon, to make the croc's tail.

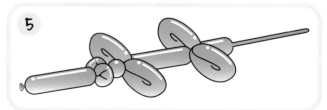

Finish the crocodile with a drawn-on face (or glue on cut-out paper eyes) and scales drawn along the tail.

Snap! Snap!

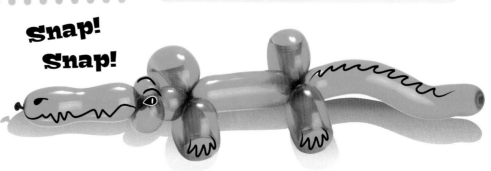

Mad, Bad Rhino

1. Begin with a bubble measuring 31 ½ in. Twist one ¾ in. bubble and two 2 in. bubbles from the knotted end to make the tail and two back legs.

2. Fold the second leg over the first and lock twist them together to the tail.

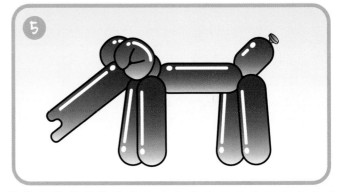

3. Twist a 2 in. bubble for the body, then twist two 2 in. bubbles for the front legs. Bend the second leg back to lock twist with the first against the body.

4. Twist a ¾ in. bubble for the neck, then a 1 ¼ in. bubble for one ear, squeezing out some air if necessary. Bend the ear back and ear twist it to the neck.

5. Twist another 1 ¼ in. bubble for the second ear. Bend it over and ear twist it into place next to the first. You should have about 4 in. of balloon left to make the head.

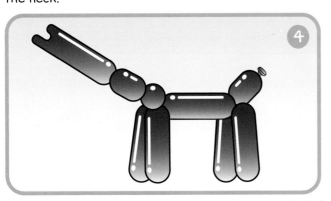

6. Grasp the head firmly and bend it down from the neck, then curve it upward. Twist the loose end of balloon round. It may take a few goes to get this right.

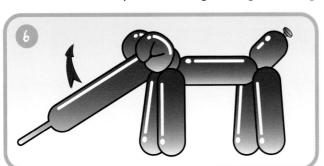

Finish off your rhinoceros with the eyes and mouth drawn in felt-tip pen.

Stomp!

Stomp!

Parrot & Swing

This model calls for brightly-colored balloons
and a colored string or ribbon to hang the swing.
Don't forget to squeeze some air out of the small bubbles.

1. Inflate a balloon to 23 1/2 in. and then twist a
1 1/4 in. bubble in the knotted end.

2. Twist a 2 in. bubble. Lock twist the knot around
this second bubble. Tuck it between the two
bubbles and hold it tight.

3. Squeeze and twist a 3/4 in. neck bubble, then two
4 in. bubbles to make the wings.

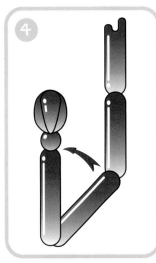

4. Lock twist the 4 in.
bubbles, then make a
further 3 3/4 in. bubble
for the parrot's body.

5. Roll the 3 3/4 in. bubble
between the two wing
bubbles. Adjust it to form
the parrot's puffed out chest.

6. Now twist two 1 1/2 in.
bubbles, bending and ear
twisting them to the body,
to form the feet. Gently
squeeze the air along the
remaining section of balloon
to make a tapering tail.

To make the parrot's swing

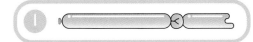

1. Inflate a balloon almost to the end.
Measure 6 in. from the knot then ear
twist a 3/4 in. bubble.

2. Ear twist a second 3/4 in. bubble
from the other end of the balloon.
Bring this bubble around to lock
twist with the knot of the balloon.

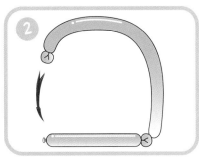

3. Adjust the shape, so that it
hangs straight, and put your parrot
in the middle of the crossbar.

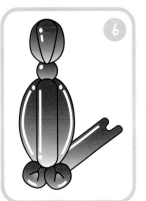

**Add drawn
eyes and claws and
hang your swing with
a ribbon.**

Bouncing Kangaroo

Red, brown or gray are good colors for this kangaroo.
Squeeze some air from the smaller bubbles
to make them easier to work.

1. Inflate a balloon to 29 ½ in. Working from the knotted end, twist a 2 in. bubble for the head.

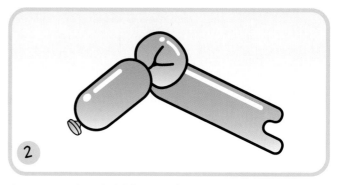

2. Twist a 1 in. bubble, bend it back and ear twist next to the head bubble.

3. Twist a second 1 in. bubble and ear twist in the same place as the first. These are the ears.

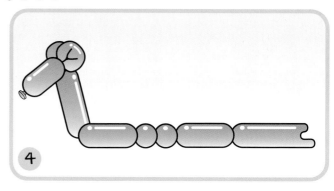

4. Now twist an 3 ¼ in. bubble for the neck, a 2 ¼ in. bubble, two ¾ in. bubbles and a further 2 ¼ in. bubble. These will form the neck, front legs and paws.

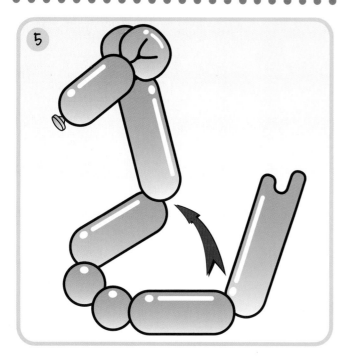

5. Lock twist the two 2 ¼ in. bubbles at the base of the neck bubble.

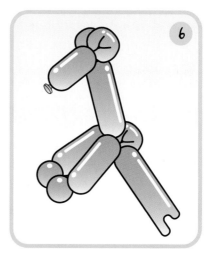

6. The next four bubbles will make the body and back legs. First, twist a 1 ¼ in. bubble, then fold it over and ear twist it at the point where the neck and front legs join.

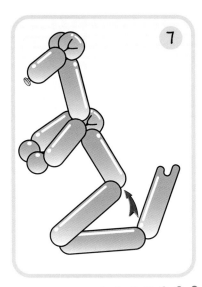

7. Twist one 3 3/4 in. bubble for the body, then two more 4 3/4 in. bubbles for back legs. Lock twist these at the base of the body.

8. Twist a 1 1/4 in. bubble, then bend it around and ear twist it to the base of the body, behind the back legs.

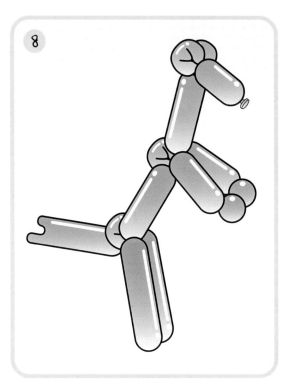

9. Squeeze the air gently along the remaining balloon to make the kangaroo's tail, curving it upward as you press. Gently curve and shape the kangaroo's body, legs and tail so that it looks good and stands upright.

Boing!
Boing!

Complete your model with eyes and a smiling mouth, drawn with a felt-tip pen—or stick on features cut from paper.

Penguin

You'll need three balloons to make this model.
Make sure you keep the leftover piece from step 1.

2. Inflate another balloon, leaving a 6 in. tip. Tie a knot in the end. Tie this knot to the knot of the beak bubble. Now pinch twist a 4 in. bubble to make the head.

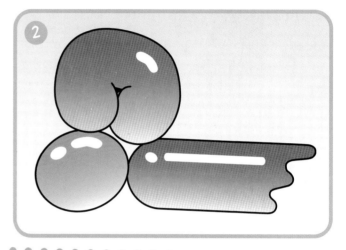

1. Inflate the beak balloon, leaving a 2 in. tip. Squeeze the air right to the end of the balloon and twist a 2 in. bubble at the tip. Holding the balloon tightly, tie a knot next to the bubble and cut a ³/₄ in. stem, saving the rest of the balloon for later.

3. Twist two 4 ³/₄ in. bubbles. Lock twist them together to make the wings. Twist a 4 in. bubble and push it between the 4 ³/₄ in. bubbles. Twist a 1 ¹/₂ in. bubble. Deflate the rest of the balloon, tie a knot and remove any surplus.

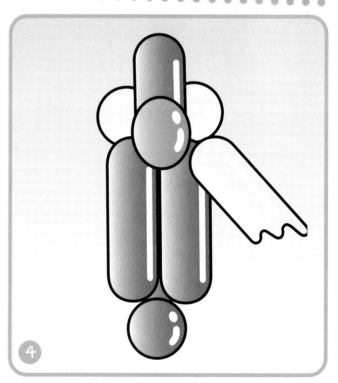

4. Inflate a third balloon, leaving a 6 in. tip. Twist two 1 ¹/₂ in. bubbles and lock twist them together. Push these bubbles through the penguin's head loop to make the cheeks.

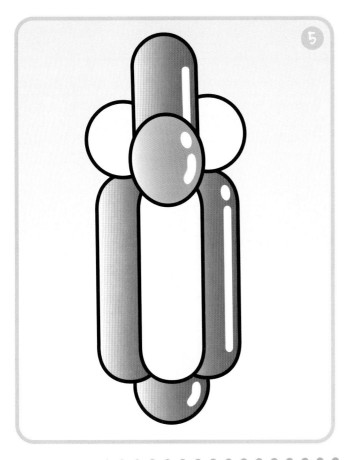

5. Twist a 4 ¾ in. bubble to make the penguin's chest. Lock twist it to the small bubble at the bottom of the body. Twist a 1 in. bubble. Holding the balloon tightly, deflate the excess, tie a knot and then cut off the end. Tuck this small bubble inside the body to secure the twists.

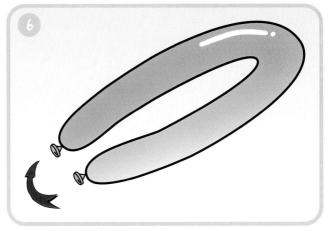

6. Make the feet from the spare piece of beak balloon. Tie a knot to seal the cut end, leaving enough stalk to tie the two knots together once you've inflated the balloon.

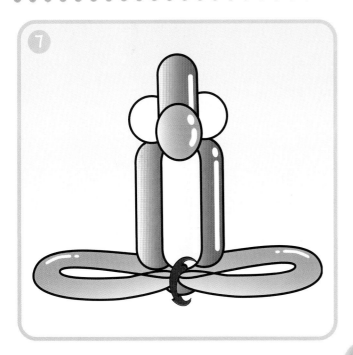

7. Twist the loop into a figure eight and lock twist the center knot around the small bubble at the base of the body.

Add eyes and a mouth with a black felt-tip pen, or glue on paper eyes and then add detail.

Elephant

Make this mighty elephant, then add it to a scene with the giraffe and crocodile (pages 14-15) for a balloon safari!

1. Inflate a balloon, leaving a 2 in. tip. Tie a knot in the end. Starting at the knotted end, twist a 7 3/4 in. bubble. Lock twist it into a loop with the knot at the end of the bubble.

2. Pass the tip of the balloon through the loop. Add a twist at the point where the balloon emerges from the loop to create the elephant's trunk. Squeeze the air along the balloon to inflate the tip, and then twist a 1 1/2 in. bubble at the end.

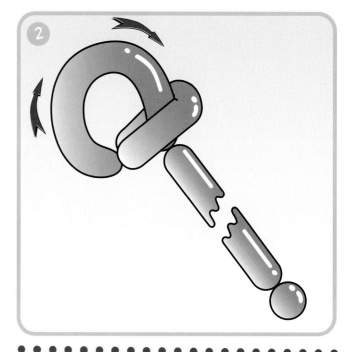

3. Make another large loop by lock twisting the 1 1/2 in. bubble to the back of the head.

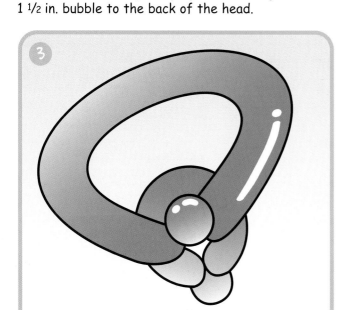

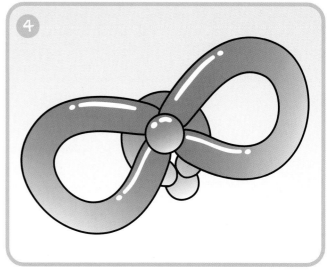

4. Press the middle of the loop down to form a figure eight and lock twist it to the 1 1/2 in. bubble.

5. Inflate another balloon, leaving a 4 in. tip. Tie a knot in the end. Starting from the knotted end, twist a 2 1/4 in. bubble for the neck. Now twist two 4 in. bubbles. Lock twist these two together to form the front legs.

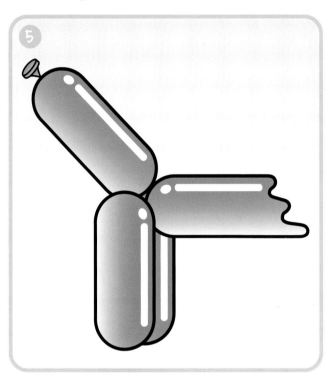

6. Twist two 4 in. bubbles and lock twist them together. Twist another 4 in. bubble and push it up between the first two to create the body.

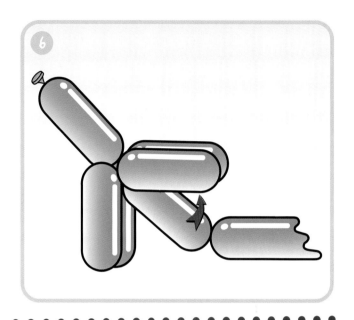

7. Lock twist two more 4 in. bubbles to make the back legs. Make the tail with a 3/4 in. bubble ear twisted close to the main body. To attach the body to the head, twist the knot of the body around the small bubble at the back of the elephant's head.

Decorate your elephant as you like. Why not try making a baby elephant too?

What next?

Now that you know how to make balloon models,
you'll probably want to try some ideas of your own!

Endless fun!

Be brave and experiment! As well as animals, you could try making numbers, letters,
trees, flowers, hats, dinosaurs and decorations. The only limit is your imagination.
Keep a handy supply of balloons and have fun!

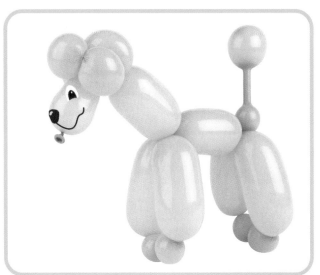